NATIONAL
GEOGRAPHIC

T0042325

People Work at the Supermarket

Felix James

I work at the supermarket. I bring food to the supermarket in a truck.

I work at the supermarket.
I unload the truck.

I work at the supermarket.
I put out the fruit.

I work at the supermarket.
I put the cans on the shelves.

I work at the supermarket.
I put meat into packages.

I work at the supermarket.
I work at the checkout.

I work at the supermarket.
I put people's food in their cars.